CW01262227

Original title:
Unfettered Heart

Copyright © 2024 Swan Charm
All rights reserved.

Author: Liisi Lendorav
ISBN HARDBACK: 978-9908-1-2164-2
ISBN PAPERBACK: 978-9908-1-2165-9
ISBN EBOOK: 978-9908-1-2166-6

An Open Invitation

Join the dance beneath the stars,
Laughter rings, no care for scars.
Colors burst, as joy aligns,
In this night, the spirit shines.

Tables laden, food to share,
Bonds of friendship fill the air.
Each heart beats in sweet refrain,
Celebrating, free from pain.

Bound to No Compass

Wandering souls beneath the moon,
Every journey sings a tune.
Paths unknown, yet spirits soar,
In every step, we seek for more.

With laughter echoing through the night,
Chasing dreams, hearts taking flight.
No map to guide, just joy in sight,
Together we embrace the light.

The Canvas of Courage

Brush in hand, we paint the sky,
Whispers of hope as colors fly.
Each stroke a tale, both brave and bold,
Festive stories waiting to unfold.

With every hue, we break the mold,
A tapestry, where hearts are sold.
Together we create the dream,
In vibrant shades, our spirits beam.

Heartbeats of the Unconfined

Feel the rhythm, pulse of life,
In every moment, joy is rife.
Hearts un tethered, dance with grace,
In this union, we find our place.

No chains to bind, we rise like mist,
In the fervor, none can resist.
Together we beat, a fierce refrain,
In the festive air, we break the chain.

Boundless Journeys

Through fields of laughter, we wander free,
With hearts aglow, and spirits in glee.
The stars above, like diamonds shine,
In this joyous dance, your hand in mine.

The road unfolds, with dreams in tow,
Each step we take, our excitement grows.
Embracing the world, with every turn,
In boundless journeys, our passions burn.

Radiance Without Restraint

With colors bursting, the skies ignite,
A symphony of joy, pure and bright.
Candles flicker with a warm embrace,
As laughter echoes in this sacred space.

With hearts unchained, we sing aloud,
Living fully, both fierce and proud.
The world is ours, let the music play,
In radiance without restraint, we sway.

Whispers of Liberation

In gentle breezes, soft whispers flow,
Tales of freedom, expecting to grow.
With every heartbeat, new dreams arise,
Echoes of promise beneath the skies.

Hands lifted high, we take a stance,
Join the rhythm, and join the dance.
With spirits soaring, no limits bind,
In whispers of liberation, souls unwind.

The Freedom Within

In moments still, our hearts align,
Discovering joys, both sweet and divine.
With every heartbeat, we find our song,
In the freedom within, we shall belong.

Breaking the chains of doubt and fear,
Embracing the now, with loved ones near.
With laughter shared, we rise and shine,
In the freedom within, our souls entwine.

Beyond the Confines

Balloons ascend, fluttering high,
Laughter echoes, reaching the sky.
Colors dance, joy fills the air,
Love surrounds us everywhere.

Candles flicker, warm evening glow,
Hope ignites, hearts all aglow.
Music swells, a joyful tune,
Under the gaze of the bright full moon.

Friends gather close, stories to share,
In these moments, nothing can compare.
Embrace the magic, let spirits soar,
In this festive realm, we crave for more.

Bound by None

Wondrous stars sprinkle the night,
Dancing flames, a whimsical sight.
Laughter rings, sparking delight,
In this freedom, everything feels right.

Shared secrets under the trees,
Gentle whispers ride the breeze.
Joyful hearts, vibrant and bright,
In unity, we find our light.

Together we rise, spirits entwined,
Celebrating life, so aligned.
With every cheer, our roots grow deep,
In this festivity, promises we keep.

The Wildness of Us

Colors swirl, a canvas of sound,
With every burst, new joys abound.
The night awakens, wild and free,
In our essence, pure jubilee.

Footsteps echo, a rhythmic dance,
In each glance, lies sweet romance.
Unruly laughter, under the stars,
Gleeful shouts from near and far.

With every moment, our spirits ignite,
Reveling in the dare of the night.
Hand in hand, we twirl and spin,
In this wildness, we all begin.

Journey to Wholeness

On this path, where laughter flows,
Festive hearts, in harmony grows.
Every step, a memory made,
In the sunlight, worries fade.

We gather 'round, our hopes aligned,
In joyful unity, love defined.
Stories exchanged, laughter and cheer,
This journey shared, treasures held dear.

With every glance, connections bloom,
Magic weaves in every room.
Together we rise, fearless and bold,
In this journey, our hearts unfold.

A Breath of Change

In the air, laughter swirls and flies,
Colors dance beneath bright blue skies.
With each cheer, hearts open wide,
Embracing moments, joy as our guide.

Candles flicker, their flames ignite,
Warming souls through the starry night.
Together we gather, hands intertwined,
A festive spirit, love unconfined.

Songs of hope ring through the crowd,
Voices lifted, vibrant and loud.
Each note carries dreams in flight,
A breath of change, pure and bright.

The Rise of Authenticity

Masks are shed in the warm soft glow,
Fears released, like seeds they sow.
Authentic smiles, no pretense here,
Celebrate the truth, let's draw near.

In the laughter, we stand tall,
No more shadows, just light for all.
Embracing flaws, we dance with grace,
This festive spirit fills the space.

With every story shared tonight,
A tapestry woven, pure delight.
Hearts united, boldly we rise,
Underneath the vast, open skies.

Veils of Complexity

Beneath bright lights, secrets unfold,
Layers sparkle like treasures of gold.
In each twist, our laughter weaves,
A festive tapestry, joy it leaves.

Moments twinkle like stars above,
We dance and share with tender love.
Through the haze, our spirits soar,
Finding magic on the dance floor.

In every glance, stories collide,
Emotions bloom, no need to hide.
Veils of complexity, gently torn,
In this festivity, we are reborn.

Realm of Unrestrained Love

In the glow of twilight's gentle embrace,
We gather together in this sacred space.
Arms open wide, hearts sing to the tune,
Of love unrestrained, beneath the moon.

Bubbles of laughter amidst joyful cheer,
Moments cherished, with all those dear.
Let the worry drift away like a dream,
In this festive realm, we shine and beam.

With every hug, warmth surrounds us all,
In this haven, we stand tall.
Unrestrained love, forever we share,
In this celebration, a world so rare.

Breaking the Mold

Stars ignite the night so bright,
Laughter dances, taking flight.
Colors burst in vibrant cheer,
Enjoy the moment, hold it near.

Joyful echoes fill the air,
Every heart is laid so bare.
Feet that shuffle, spirits bold,
Together breaking the old mold.

Unleashed Desires

Whispers sweet like summer blooms,
All around, the music zooms.
Hearts awaken, passions flare,
In the night, the dreamers dare.

Once restrained, now spirits fly,
Underneath the painted sky.
Every wish, a fire ignites,
Unleashed desires, joyful nights.

Hearts Apart

Underneath the twinkling lights,
We share our dreams on starry nights.
Distance lingers, but hope stays near,
Hearts apart, yet crystal clear.

Messages in bottles cast,
Carried whispers of the past.
Love transcends each time and space,
In every smile, we find our grace.

Souls Together

Fingers woven, tightly bound,
In this circle, love is found.
Simple joys, we celebrate,
Souls together, hearts elate.

From every corner, voices blend,
In this moment, all amend.
Lively chants and laughter soar,
Unified, we crave for more.

The Infinite Pulse

Heartbeat echoes through the crowd,
In this rhythm, proud and loud.
Moments merge, lives intertwine,
The infinite pulse, so divine.

Sound and sight in harmony,
Joyful faces, pure esprit.
Together we create and thrive,
In every beat, we come alive.

Echoes of the Untamed

In the heart of the meadow, joy does spring,
Laughter twirls like a bright, golden thing.
Colors burst forth in a radiant display,
Nature's own music invites us to play.

Wildflowers blooming, beneath the sun's gaze,
Sing to the rhythm of life's vivid blaze.
A tapestry woven with threads of delight,
Echoes of freedom dance into the night.

Unleashed Echoes

From the depths of the forest, voices arise,
Whispers of wonder beneath open skies.
The air is electric, alive with the sound,
Unleashed echoes of joy all around.

With every heartbeat, the world comes alive,
In unity's warmth, together we thrive.
Dancing and spinning, we let spirits soar,
Unleashed echoes that beckon for more.

The Dance of Liberation

Under bright lanterns, shadows do sway,
We gather together, come join the play.
With each twirl and leap, our souls intertwine,
In this dance of liberation, our spirits align.

The drums beat a rhythm, strong and free,
A celebration of life, just you and me.
Hand in hand, we break every chain,
In the dance of liberation, we lose all pain.

Serendipity's Call

The sun dips low, painting skies in gold,
A moment of magic, the stories unfold.
In laughter and joy, we find our own way,
Serendipity's call fills the air with play.

In the twinkle of lights, friendship ignites,
As stars start to shimmer on velvety nights.
We gather in circles, stories to share,
With serendipity's call, there's magic in the air.

Navigating Open Skies

Balloons rise high in the glow,
Children laugh, faces aglow.
Laughter dances in the air,
Joyful moments, none to spare.

Colors swirl like a warm embrace,
Friends unite in a bustling space.
Songs of freedom fill the land,
Hearts entwined, hand in hand.

Banners wave in the soft breeze,
Echoed cheer among the trees.
Bright lights twinkle through the night,
Every gaze fixed on the bright.

Under stars, stories unfold,
Adventures waiting to be told.
With every dream that softly flies,
We celebrate beneath open skies.

The Call of the Infinite

A melody floats above the crowd,
Songs of starlight, sweet and loud.
Each note resonates with delight,
Guiding souls into the night.

Sky lanterns drift, a soft embrace,
Every heart finds its right place.
Connection sparkles, strong and true,
In this moment, me and you.

Whispers of dreams, woven with care,
In every breath, a fragrant air.
We share the rhythm of the day,
Chasing worries far away.

As the dusk turns to dawn's clear light,
We dance in laughter, pure and bright.
Infinite joy fills every space,
Together, we find our place.

Beyond the Barrier

The gate swings wide, a world in bloom,
Hope and laughter chase away gloom.
Faces shine with eager grace,
Secrets shared in a brightened space.

Children's giggles rise like dew,
With each moment, something new.
Joyful echoes fill the streets,
Every rhythm, heartbeats meet.

Fleeting dreams on the vibrant ground,
In their laughter, life is found.
Colors blend and cultures merge,
In this fiesta, spirits surge.

We break the walls that hold us tight,
United in this shared delight.
As one we stand, our hearts set free,
Beyond the barrier, just you and me.

The Essence of Release

In the dusk, colors set ablaze,
Hearts unbound in the twilight haze.
Laughter spills, chasing the dark,
Moments ignited, each a spark.

Candles glow with hopeful flames,
We come together, calling names.
Every hug, a gentle embrace,
In the warmth of this sacred space.

Time suspended, lost in cheer,
The essence of love, crystal clear.
Every voice blends in the air,
A tapestry of joy to share.

As night blankets our vibrant land,
We gather close, hand in hand.
In this revelry, we take flight,
Celebrating the essence of light.

A Journey Beyond Chains

In the light of the moon, we dance with glee,
With laughter and joy, we set our hearts free.
Stars twinkle bright, guiding us away,
From shadows of doubt, into the day.

With colors ablaze, our spirits ignite,
We celebrate life, glowing so bright.
The chains of the past, we leave far behind,
In the warmth of the now, new dreams we find.

Through valleys of hope, we wander and roam,
In a world full of wonder, we create our home.
With every new step, the rhythm we bring,
Life is a melody; we dance and we sing.

Together we rise, hand in hand we soar,
In a journey of heart, we are evermore.
With the wind in our hair, and joy in our hearts,
This journey beyond chains, a celebration starts.

Embrace the Wild

Underneath the sun, where the wild things play,
We gather together, to laugh and to sway.
Nature sings sweetly, her voice a soft tune,
As we embrace her, beneath the warm moon.

With each breath we take, we join in the fun,
With every heartbeat, we dance as one.
The whispers of freedom, they call out our name,
In the wild, we find joy, and life is our game.

Gather 'round the fire, stories we share,
The flickering flames, a warm, loving glare.
We toast to the night, with laughter and cheer,
In the wild, we are free, with nothing to fear.

With arms open wide, we welcome the stars,
In the embrace of the wild, we heal all our scars.
Together we soar, to the beat of our hearts,
In this moment of joy, our adventure starts.

Heart Unchained

A heart unchained, it dances with grace,
In the rhythm of life, we all find our place.
With smiles so bright, we light up the night,
In this boundless space, everything feels right.

We frolic through fields, under skies painted gold,
Each moment a treasure, a story retold.
Voices harmonize, like birds on the wing,
In the joy of our laughter, we find freedom's swing.

Hands clasped together, we lift our song high,
With dreams as our wings, we reach for the sky.
In the warmth of each heart, a fire ignites,
Uniting us all, in these beautiful nights.

A tapestry woven, of love and of cheer,
In the dance of freedom, we have nothing to fear.
With our hearts unchained, we soar and we shine,
In this festive embrace, your heart is with mine.

The Rhythm of Freedom

In the pulse of the night, a rhythm is born,
With drums of joy, we greet the dawn.
A symphony plays, wild winds invite,
As we lose ourselves in the dance of light.

In corners of laughter, the music flows free,
When hearts come together, pure harmony.
With each joyful step, our spirits take flight,
In the rhythm of freedom, everything feels right.

The colors of life swirl around with delight,
A canvas of joy, in the magical night.
Beneath twinkling stars, we break from the chains,
In the dance of our dreams, true magic remains.

So let us celebrate, hand in hand through the night,
In the rhythm of freedom, our souls shine bright.
With laughter and love, we'll dance and we'll sing,
In the heart of the moment, true joy is the king.

Chains of Affection

In the glow of lantern light,
We gather close, hearts in flight.
Laughter dances in the air,
Joyful whispers everywhere.

Hands entwined, a vivid thread,
Stories shared, no words unsaid.
Love's embrace, a warm cocoon,
Together we sing to the moon.

Candles flicker, spirits soar,
Every moment, we ask for more.
In this unity, we find our song,
Forever, in this dance, we belong.

Boundless Beat

Drums are thumping, hearts collide,
In this rhythm, we take pride.
Feet are moving, feelings high,
Underneath the starry sky.

Colors flashing, smiles abound,
In the music, love is found.
Every heartbeat syncs in time,
Together making life a rhyme.

Voices rise, a joyful cheer,
Spirits free, we have no fear.
In this moment, we are one,
Dancing 'til the night is done.

Wings of Vulnerability

With open hearts, we take a chance,
In this circle, we all dance.
Sharing dreams, our souls laid bare,
Finding strength in tender care.

Every tear, a seed of grace,
Blooming joy in this safe space.
Hands reaching out, we lift each other,
In this tapestry, we discover.

Colors blend, we paint the sky,
Courage soaring, learning to fly.
In this freedom, we become bright,
Wings of love take joyful flight.

Breath of Liberation

As dawn breaks, we greet the day,
A new beginning, come what may.
Joyful laughter fills the air,
In this moment, we lay bare.

Hands held high, we celebrate,
Casting off the chains of fate.
Every heartbeat, a song of cheer,
With every breath, we draw you near.

Shadows fade, and light shines through,
In this space, we start anew.
Hearts unbound, we'll reach the sun,
In unity, we're never done.

Love's Untamed Journey

Through valleys wide, we dance and play,
With laughter bright, we greet the day.
Our spirits soar like birds in flight,
In love's embrace, we shine so bright.

A river flows, with dreams untold,
In every heartbeat, warmth and gold.
Together we sail on waves of bliss,
Each moment a treasure, a gentle kiss.

The stars above, they twinkle clear,
With every glance, I hold you near.
In tangled paths, our fates entwined,
A symphony of hearts, forever designed.

In gardens wild, where roses bloom,
We carve our story, dispelling gloom.
With each embrace, the world ignites,
In love's untamed journey, hope ignites.

Wildfire of Emotion

Like flames that dance in summer's breeze,
Our love ignites with fiery ease.
Each glance a spark, each touch a flare,
In wild abandon, we lay bare.

With laughter ringing through the night,
We chase the shadows, holding tight.
A whirlwind force, so fierce, so bright,
In passion's grip, we take our flight.

In every heartbeat, sparks alive,
Our souls entwined, our spirits thrive.
The world a canvas, painted bold,
With strokes of joy, our tale unfolds.

As embers glow beneath the moon,
We share our secrets, hearts in tune.
In this dance of fire, we reside,
In wildfire of emotion, love won't hide.

Heartstrings Unchained

With every note, our hearts align,
In melodies sweet, our souls entwine.
Through music's pulse, we find our way,
In harmony's arms, we dance and sway.

The rhythm calls, a lively beat,
In laughter's echo, our worlds meet.
Joyous whispers wrap around,
In heartstrings unchained, love is found.

As colors burst in vibrant hues,
We paint our dreams with love's own muse.
In every moment, pure delight,
Our hearts in chorus, day and night.

Together we weave a tapestry,
Of endless laughter, wild and free.
In this embrace, we rise, we reign,
Forever bound in heartstrings unchained.

The Open Veins of Passion

In twilight's glow, our passions bloom,
With every heartbeat, dispelling gloom.
The night ignites, our spirits race,
In open veins, we find our place.

Each whispered word, a tender fire,
Your gaze a spark, my heart's desire.
With every touch, the world ignites,
In fervent dance, we claim the nights.

Through shadows deep, we boldly stride,
In passion's flame, we will not hide.
With open hearts, we dare to dream,
United in love, a boundless stream.

In this embrace, forever bold,
Our story whispered, softly told.
The open veins of passion's art,
A canvas painted from the heart.

Threads of Infinite Dreams

In the shimmer of twilight's embrace,
Colors dance in a joyous race.
Laughter rings under starlit skies,
Hope flickers bright, never dies.

Balloons drift high, carried on air,
Magic swirls in the hearts we share.
Candles flicker, their glow inviting,
Wishes soar, ever exciting.

Children's giggles blend with the night,
Embracing dreams, the future is bright.
Together we weave tales of delight,
Under the moon, our spirits take flight.

A Heart's Odyssey

In a world painted with vibrant hues,
We gather, exchanging joyous news.
A symphony of hearts, they beat,
Dancing to rhythms, oh so sweet.

Through winding paths, our laughter flows,
A tapestry of friendship grows.
In every song, our spirits rise,
Revelations found in each surprise.

Hands held tight, we sail through time,
In the embrace of love's soft chime.
Every moment a treasure we find,
In this odyssey, hearts intertwined.

Beyond the Walls of Silence

Whispers echo in the twilight glow,
Where laughter blooms, and friendships grow.
Beneath the stars, we craft our fate,
In this realm, where dreams await.

Glimmers of joy in every glance,
A festival of souls in a dance.
We break the silence, sing our song,
Together we flourish, forever strong.

From shadowed corners, joy emerges,
A river of hope that gently surges.
With hearts as lanterns, lighting the way,
We celebrate life, come what may.

Love's Frontier

Beneath a sky adorned with gold,
Stories of love and laughter unfold.
In every heartbeat, a spark ignites,
A festive spirit that never fights.

We sail on echoes of song and cheer,
Embracing the moments we hold dear.
Every smile a promise, warm and bright,
Guiding our souls like stars in the night.

Across the fields where joy abounds,
In the magic of love, our happiness found.
Together we journey, side by side,
In love's frontier, where dreams abide.

Spirit Unbound

Joyful laughter fills the air,
Colors dance in sunlight's glare.
Friends unite, hands reach out,
Celebration's what it's about.

Candles flicker, wishes soar,
Music calls us to the floor.
Heartbeats sync in rhythm's sway,
Together we chase dusk away.

Starlit skies, a canvas bright,
Dreams take wing in pure delight.
In this moment, hearts connect,
Spirit unbound, we reflect.

Every smile, a spark divine,
Unity in every line.
The world is ours, the night is free,
In this fest, just you and me.

Hearts Without Borders

Underneath a moonlit sky,
We share stories, letting fly.
Voices blend, a heartfelt song,
In this space, where we belong.

From every corner, we convene,
With open hearts, a vibrant scene.
Cultures mix, traditions blend,
In this journey, love won't end.

Laughter echoes, bright and clear,
Bridge of dreams, we hold so dear.
Hand in hand, we dance, we sing,
In our unity, we take wing.

With every step, we break the mold,
Stories shared, a joy untold.
Hearts without borders, bold and free,
In this tapestry, you and me.

Emancipated Echoes

Freedom rings in joyous tones,
Every heart beats like a drum.
Echoes of laughter fill the space,
Together, we embrace the grace.

Time to celebrate, to rejoice,
In our freedom, we find our voice.
Songs of old mix with the new,
In this moment, we all break through.

Colors twirl in vibrant streams,
Dancing shadows cast our dreams.
Footsteps weave a tale so bright,
Emancipated, pure delight.

Lift your spirits, let them soar,
In this bond, we ask for more.
Together on this joyful trek,
We find our strength in what we reflect.

The Dance of Freedom

With the dawn, a new sun shines,
In our laughter, love entwines.
Feet on earth, our spirits rise,
In the rhythm, freedom lies.

Colors swirl, a joyous sight,
Hearts ignite in pure delight.
From the shadows, we emerge,
In this dance, we feel the urge.

Every twirl, a song we make,
Together, we are wide awake.
In the circle, hands are held,
In this moment, we're compelled.

As the stars begin to glow,
We connect, we ebb and flow.
In the dance, our dreams are spun,
Celebrating all that's begun.

Heartstrings Unbound

In the air, laughter rings,
As every joy, the heart brings.
Colors dance in vibrant hues,
Life's a festival, we choose.

Friends and family gather near,
With every toast, we share cheer.
Songs of love fill up the night,
Our spirits soar, hearts take flight.

Candles flicker, shadows play,
Moments weave, come what may.
Stories old, yet forever new,
Together here, just me and you.

Under stars, we raise our glass,
Let worries fade, let troubles pass.
Hearts entwined, unbound we stand,
In this realm, all dreams are planned.

Soaring Without Limits

Beneath the sky, the kites ascend,
With every breath, the world we mend.
Laughter echoes, dreams take flight,
In this moment, all feels right.

Hands held tight, we spin and twirl,
In joy's embrace, our hearts unfurl.
Every smile, a spark divine,
In the glow, our spirits shine.

Underneath the glimmering stars,
Boundless dreams, no need for bars.
With every heartbeat, we explore,
In festive joy, we crave for more.

With friends beside, we find our way,
In this revelry, let's laugh and play.
Together stronger, side by side,
In this vast world, it's love we ride.

The Invincible Pulse

In vibrant beats, the music flows,
With every step, excitement grows.
The dance begins, hearts race anew,
In the rhythm, we break through.

Fireworks burst in the night sky,
Each color sings a joyful hi.
The world alights in festive cheer,
With open arms, we gather near.

Every moment, a memory made,
In this light, we're unafraid.
Chasing dreams, together we run,
Under the moon, we are all one.

With hearts ablaze, we paint the air,
In joyous tunes, we shed our cares.
Together we laugh, together we sing,
In this circle, we find our wings.

Where the Heart Dares

In hidden corners, laughter swells,
Where the heart dares, joy compels.
Each whispered dream, a spark of hope,
In this wide world, together we cope.

As daylight fades, the stars awake,
With every wish, our souls we stake.
Festive tales of old and new,
In stories shared, our hearts break through.

Around the fire, warmth surrounds,
In its glow, the love abounds.
Every moment, precious and rare,
In this grand dance, we have no care.

With freedom's song in every sway,
Where the heart dares, we find our way.
Together united, we forge ahead,
In festive spirits, our dreams are fed.

Tides of True Desire

Waves crash with a jubilant cheer,
Whispers of passion fill the air.
Stars twinkle in a dance of delight,
Hearts entwined, glowing bright.

In every pulse, a heartbeat sings,
Moments shared, like vibrant springs.
The lanterns glow with wishes near,
Embracing love devoid of fear.

Colors merge, and laughter flows,
In this tide, true desire grows.
Hands are held, and spirits soar,
Together, we yearn for more.

As the moonlight paints the scene,
Alive with joy, we live the dream.
In this dance, forever bound,
In tides of love, we are found.

Awakening Raw Truths

The sun breaks through the morning haze,
With every line, the truth displays.
Voices rise like banners high,
In unity, we touch the sky.

With every laugh, we shed the past,
In vibrant moments, we hold fast.
The world around us spins and twirls,
In raw truths, our flag unfurls.

Colors blend in rich exchange,
Hearts enlightened, thoughts arrange.
In every smile, a story's told,
Awakening truths, brave and bold.

Hand in hand, we break the mold,
In every warmth, a spark unfolds.
Together, we chase the light,
Awakening visions, pure delight.

Opalescent Dreams

In a realm where colors gleam,
We wander through opalescent dreams.
Wonders bloom with every sigh,
A canvas painted by the sky.

Glistening trails of silver and gold,
Stories whispered, secrets told.
With every step, we dance in light,
Shimmering shadows, pure delight.

The air is filled with joy unbound,
In this moment, love is found.
Gaze into the depths of night,
Opalescent dreams take flight.

A vibrant world, forever bright,
Hearts ablaze, igniting the night.
In this journey, together we gleam,
Lost in our opalescent dream.

The Melody of Release

Notes cascade like falling rain,
In melodies, we break the chain.
Voices soaring, spirits free,
In this song, we find our glee.

Harmonies weave through the air,
Lifting hearts without a care.
The rhythm dances in the night,
Together, we embrace the light.

With every beat, we shed our fears,
In joyous laughter, we hold dear.
The melody wraps us in grace,
As we move to a timeless place.

In this symphony of release,
Our souls entwined, we find our peace.
Together, we chant and cheer,
In the melody, love draws near.

Unbridled Dreams

In a world where laughter rings,
We dance 'neath the vibrant stars,
With every hope the heart brings,
We paint our joy on night's bars.

Glimmers of wishes take flight,
As confetti showers us down,
With friends gathered, hearts so light,
The spirit of joy wears a crown.

Each moment a treasure to share,
A tapestry woven with cheer,
Life bursts forth, a colorful flare,
In this festive time of the year.

Together we sing and we sway,
Embracing the warmth of the night,
With unbridled dreams on display,
Our hearts shining ever so bright.

A Symphony of Release

The drums beat in rhythmic delight,
While voices rise, a chorus of cheer,
Melodies dancing in soft twilight,
Each note a whisper we hold dear.

Hands lifted high, we unite,
In a wave of passion, we soar,
With every laugh, we ignite,
A symphony we all explore.

Cinnamon scents fill the air,
As laughter spills, a joyous blend,
With every moment a flair,
Together, our hearts transcend.

The music wraps 'round like a warm hug,
Caressing each soul with its grace,
In this symphony, we snug,
Finding freedom in every place.

Cascades of Authenticity

With laughter that echoes near,
We gather in circles bright,
Embracing our truth, no fear,
In the glow of the moonlight.

Stories woven in the breeze,
As hearts share their tales unbound,
Together, we create with ease,
Cascades of joy all around.

Colors burst like spring's first bloom,
Truth sparkles in every glance,
In this festive, vibrant room,
We find our rhythm, our dance.

With voices raised, we belong,
In the chorus of love's decree,
In authenticity, we are strong,
Together, we celebrate free.

Flight of the Fearless

The night ignites with bright delight,
As we gather, bold and true,
Chasing dreams with all our might,
Underneath the stars so blue.

With every step, we embrace,
The thrill of life, wild and free,
In the echo of joy's face,
We glide on wings, daring to be.

Fearless, we leap into the air,
The world spins in festive cheer,
Together, we conquer despair,
With love, our hearts adhere.

In this celebration of flight,
We dance with the fireflies' light,
With laughter that fills the night,
The spirit of joy feels just right.

The Road to Wholeness

On the road where laughter sings,
Joy spills over like bright springs.
Steps like petals, soft and light,
Facing warmth from morning's bright.

Gathered hands in circles wide,
Dance of souls, all hearts allied.
Stars above in glowing cheer,
Every whisper, love draws near.

Painted skies and colors blend,
Each new breath, a hopeful mend.
Winding paths and open doors,
In this journey, spirit soars.

Together on this vibrant quest,
Where every heart reveals its best.
In unity, we find our way,
Celebrating life's grand ballet.

Embracing the Unknown

In shadows cast by moonlit beams,
We dance along with daring dreams.
Hearts aflame, igniting souls,
In the unknown, each one unfolds.

Whispers beckon, urging flight,
On this path, we blaze with light.
Fear dissolves like evening mist,
In this moment, joy can't be missed.

Every mystery holds a key,
Unlocking realms of ecstasy.
With each step, we boldly stride,
Embracing what the fates decide.

Together we will face the tide,
With laughter as our faithful guide.
In the dance of life, we play,
Finding bliss in every sway.

Caress of Liberation

With open arms, the winds do sing,
In every heart, a fire takes wing.
Boundless dreams soar through the air,
In liberation, we find our care.

Songs of freedom, echoes sweet,
Rhythms pulse in every beat.
Wild and free, we chase the night,
Together in the pure delight.

Moments cherished, vibrant glow,
In the caress, we learn and grow.
With each laugh, let burdens fade,
In unity, we break the braid.

An endless sky, a canvas bright,
Embracing all, a shared insight.
In the dance of life, we'll soar,
Finding joy forevermore.

Horizons of Passion

Where the sun kisses the sea,
Waves of passion set us free.
In the moment, love takes flight,
Painting dreams in colors bright.

Each heartbeat sings a vibrant tune,
Underneath the silver moon.
Sparkling eyes and soft caress,
In this magic, we are blessed.

With open hearts, we greet the dawn,
In the dance of life, we're drawn.
Horizons beckon, wide and true,
In shared laughter, me and you.

Bursting forth, we claim our space,
In every smile, a warm embrace.
Together on this journey vast,
In passion's grip, our spells are cast.

Echoing Through the Void

In the night, bells chime bright,
Stars dance with pure delight,
Whispers of joy fill the air,
Together, we banish despair.

Voices rise, a song of cheer,
Every heart feels the near,
Colors swirl, laughter flows,
A tapestry of love that grows.

With every beat, we unite,
In this moment, we're alight,
Echoing joy, every sound,
In this void, hope is found.

A Song for the Unchained

Freedom breathes with every note,
Spirits dance, take to the boat,
On rivers of dreams, we glide,
In harmony, we take pride.

Chains are broken, hearts take flight,
Together we bask in the light,
With every moment, we rejoice,
In the rhythm, we find our voice.

The melody calls, hear it sing,
In this gathering, we are kings,
A symphony of love to share,
Unchained souls, beyond compare.

Unwinding the Heart

In soft hues of golden light,
We gather close, hearts feel right,
Unraveling stories, laughter spills,
Joyous echoes across the hills.

As time drips like honey sweet,
With every heartbeat, we repeat,
The dance of life, so vibrant, clear,
A tapestry woven with cheer.

With open arms, we embrace,
In this moment, find our place,
Unwinding fears, we're set free,
Together, how sweet harmony.

The Light of Anew

Morning breaks with sparkling rays,
A new dawn brings brighter days,
We celebrate, the world aglow,
In this warmth, our spirits flow.

Candles flicker, colors burst,
In this moment, love is first,
Whispers of hope dance in the air,
Together, we conquer despair.

With every smile, the world awakes,
A joyous journey, on love it takes,
The light of anew fills our hearts,
Together, we'll never part.

Where the Heart Roams

In the glow of lantern lights, warm and bright,
Laughter dances on the breeze tonight.
Joyful echoes fill the air,
As hearts entwine without a care.

Underneath the stars' soft gleam,
We chase the magic, chase the dream.
With every step, our spirits soar,
Together, we'll explore even more.

In bustling streets and laughter's song,
In every moment, we belong.
Embracing life, so rich and sweet,
Where the heart roams, love is complete.

Serendipity's Embrace

A serendipitous twist of fate,
With every smile, we celebrate.
The universe whispers secrets true,
In colors bright, and skies so blue.

Dancing shadows in the twilight glow,
Our hearts entwined, a wondrous flow.
With every laughter, hope ignites,
As day transforms to vibrant nights.

In this embrace of laughter and light,
We find ourselves in pure delight.
Hand in hand, we take a chance,
In joy's embrace, we leap and dance.

The Courage to Feel

With courage blooms the heart's delight,
In colors bold, we shed the night.
A tapestry of joy we weave,
In every moment, we believe.

We brave the laughter, we brave the tears,
Celebrating life throughout the years.
With every heartbeat, we reveal,
The tender strength in the courage to feel.

In vibrant tunes, our spirits rise,
Beneath a canvas of painted skies.
We cherish moments, fleeting yet real,
In the beauty of life, we learn to feel.

Echoes of the Untamed

In forests deep, the wild winds roam,
Whispering tales of nature's home.
Echoes call from tree to glen,
A dance of life, again and again.

Each rustling leaf sings freedom's song,
In unity, we all belong.
Underneath the moon's soft gaze,
We find our rhythm in nature's maze.

With joyful hearts, we leap and play,
Savoring the magic of each new day.
Embracing the pulse of earth's refrain,
We celebrate echoes of the untamed.

Flames of Connection

In a circle of laughter we stand,
With our hearts aglow, hand in hand.
Each smile ignites the warmth we share,
Together we dance, free from all care.

The music swells, a vibrant cheer,
With every note, we pull each near.
Boundless joy fills the evening light,
In this sacred space, everything feels right.

As the night deepens, our spirits soar,
Stories and dreams flow from core to core.
The fire flickers, casting shadows wide,
In the flames of connection, we all confide.

With each spark that rises high,
We celebrate moments that never die.
A warmth that lingers, a bond that stays,
In hearts and souls, through all our days.

A Tapestry of Freedom

Bright colors weave through open skies,
Each thread of laughter, where freedom lies.
A tapestry rich with dreams and cheer,
Celebrating all we hold dear.

The wind whispers secrets of yore,
Under the stars, we ask for more.
With every whisper, a promise we make,
In this festivity, our spirits awake.

We gather in unity, hand in hand,
Together we rise, a vibrant band.
Freedom shines in the dawn's embrace,
As we twirl and revel in this sacred space.

The joy of being, a dance that unfolds,
A tapestry woven with dreams so bold.
In this moment, we freely roam,
Creating together our cherished home.

Shores of Infinite Possibility

Upon the shores where the waves crash bright,
We gather our hopes to take flight.
With laughter ringing like the sea's song,
In this ocean of joy, we all belong.

The sun paints gold on the water's face,
Each step we take, we embrace the grace.
The horizon beckons, a canvas wide,
Where dreams and wishes in waves collide.

We build our castles, with sand and delight,
Crafting our futures in the morning light.
In each heart, a spark ignites,
In the shores of possibility, our spirit invites.

As we dance in the tides, feeling alive,
Stories and laughter together we strive.
These shores, a haven for all we pursue,
In this endless realm, we create anew.

The Flow of Honest Emotion

In the rhythm of music, we lose our fears,
Emotions flowing like rivers of tears.
With every beat, our hearts align,
In this festive space, we intertwine.

Expressions sparkle in the glowing lights,
As we share our stories, chasing heights.
Honesty blooms in every word spoken,
In connections forged, no heart left broken.

Laughter erupts and sorrows release,
In the dance of feelings, we find our peace.
With open arms, we welcome the night,
In this flow of emotion, everything feels right.

Together we rise, united in joy,
Each moment cherished, nothing can cloy.
In the circle of trust, we find our way,
Celebrating differences, come what may.

The Art of Letting Go

In the air, bright colors sway,
Laughter dances, come what may.
Wishes whispered in the breeze,
Hearts unburdened, minds at ease.

Hands released, we bloom and grow,
Joyful spirits, ebb and flow.
With each moment, let it be,
Embrace the bliss of being free.

Serenade of the Free

Under stars, the music swells,
Notes of freedom, ringing bells.
Voices lift like birds in flight,
Chasing dreams into the night.

Every heartbeat, a sweet refrain,
Echoing through sun and rain.
Together in this vibrant choir,
Melodies spark a glowing fire.

Garden of Willing Hearts

In the garden, love abounds,
Every petal softly sounds.
Laughing faces, smiles unfold,
Stories shared, both new and old.

Colors merge, in sweet embrace,
Life's gentle touch, a warm grace.
Hopes planted deep, roots intertwine,
In this haven, all is fine.

The Joy of Untethered Souls

With the dawn, our spirits rise,
Chasing joy beneath the skies.
Unchained laughter, pure delight,
Dancing shadows, soft moonlight.

In this freedom, we are whole,
Every moment feeds the soul.
Together we shall take a chance,
In this life, we'll boldly dance.

Heartbeats of Independence

In the air, bright colors soar,
Laughter echoes, spirits adore.
Flags waving high in jubilant cheer,
Together we stand, united and clear.

Fireworks burst like vivid dreams,
In the night, joy's laughter gleams.
Hearts race as the anthem plays,
Celebrating hope in diverse ways.

Beneath the stars, voices unite,
A dance of freedom, shining bright.
Each heartbeat sings a patriotic tune,
Beneath the watchful, glowing moon.

Together in warmth, a festival grand,
We share this gift, hand in hand.
Independence blooms, joy runs deep,
In our hearts forever to keep.

A Canvas of Longing

Brushstrokes of dreams against the night,
Pulsing softly, a glowing light.
Colors blend in whispers sweet,
Painting visions of souls that meet.

Glimmers of hope in every hue,
Awaiting a love that feels so true.
In this silence, the heartbeats play,
A canvas alive, where wishes stay.

Each stroke a tale, a moment caught,
In the gallery of longing, love is sought.
As the brush dances, emotions rise,
Creating a world that never lies.

The masterpiece, a heartbeat's song,
In dreams of belonging, we all belong.
Framed in the joy of what could be,
A canvas of longing, forever free.

The Uncharted Path

Wanderers tread on roads unknown,
With each step, new seeds are sown.
Through lush valleys and peaks of fire,
Hope ignites as dreams inspire.

Footprints left in whispers' grace,
In every turn, a sacred space.
The heart leads on, no map in hand,
Navigating a vast, wild land.

Sunlight glimmers through the trees,
Dancing leaves on the gentle breeze.
With open hearts, we journey on,
Each path we take, our fears are gone.

In the wild unknown, we find our way,
Embracing life's vibrant ballet.
Together we roam, spirits aligned,
In the uncharted, new worlds unwind.

Dancing Between Freedom and Fear

Under starlit skies, we sway,
In shadows where hope finds its way.
The rhythm pulses, a beat we share,
Balancing grace with a hint of dare.

In the tension, we find our light,
Fear whispered low, freedom ignites.
With every step, we chase the night,
Dancing boldly, hearts taking flight.

We whirl through doubts, yet we press on,
In vibrant chaos, we find our song.
Fear may linger but fades with cheer,
For in our hearts, love conquers fear.

Together we dance in the sacred space,
Embracing the beauty of this wild race.
Between freedom's call and fleeting dread,
In the dance of life, fear's gently shed.

Free to Roam

In the sun's warm embrace, we dance with glee,
Laughter rings out, wild and free,
Colors twirl in the joyful air,
Together we roam, without a care.

The world unfolds, a canvas bright,
With friends beside, hearts take flight,
Every step a song, a vibrant tune,
Under the watchful, gleaming moon.

Carrying dreams on the breeze we chase,
A rhythm of joy, a symphonic place,
With every heartbeat, we sing our song,
A tapestry woven where we all belong.

In this moment, we feel alive,
In the spirit of love, we thrive,
Let's paint the sky with our delight,
Together we'll shine, a beacon of light.

Wings of Desire

Beneath the stars, we rise and soar,
With hopes like feathers, we long for more,
The night is alive with whispers sweet,
Dancing on dreams, our hearts will meet.

Candles flicker in the gentle breeze,
Laughter spills like a melody that frees,
The world ignites with colorful flames,
In the warmth of friendship, no one is to blame.

Oh, these wings, they carry our wishes,
Through the air, like soft summer swishes,
We'll paint the skies, let our spirits glide,
With the moon as our guide, in joy we'll abide.

As the music plays, let worries fade,
With every note, a serenade,
In this festive realm where dreams transpire,
Together forever, on wings of desire.

Boundless Aspirations

With every dawn, new dreams unfold,
In a world of wonder, stories told,
We chase the sunlight, hand in hand,
Carving our paths in golden sand.

Voices rise in a jubilant cheer,
In the heart of the fest, we conquer fear,
Every heartbeat echoes our tale,
Carried by hope, we shall not fail.

The colors of life paint our desires,
With laughter and love, we build our fires,
Reaching for stars that light the night,
In boundless skies, we take flight.

Together we stand, our spirits bright,
In the warmth of the day, through the cool of night,
With aspirations high, we claim our fate,
In this festive journey, we create.

Whispers of Liberation

In the soft glow of this festive night,
We cast away shadows, embrace the light,
Each laugh a note in our joyful song,
Together we rise, where we all belong.

Whispers of freedom dance in the air,
In our hearts, a secret we share,
With every twirl, we break our chains,
In the rhythm of life, love reigns.

The stars envelop us, dreams take flight,
Through the darkness, we shine so bright,
Bound by our laughter, our spirits soar,
In this moment, we yearn for more.

With arms wide open, we greet the dawn,
In the tapestry of life, we're drawn,
Whispers of liberation, let them rise,
In the harmony of love, we'll touch the skies.

A Symphony of Release

In a garden bright, colors blend,
Laughter echoes, voices ascend.
With every note, joy takes flight,
Under the stars, through the night.

Balloons rise high, dreams unfurl,
As twinkling lights begin to swirl.
Hands join together in pure delight,
Hearts beating loud, everything feels right.

The music swells, a dance begins,
Spinning and twirling, lose the sins.
Fingers snap, the rhythm's sweet,
In this moment, feel the heartbeat.

Celebrate now, let worries cease,
In this symphony, find your peace.
With friends around, spirits ignite,
A night of wonder, pure and bright.

Flight of the Heart

Wings of laughter lift us high,
Beneath the canvas of the sky.
With every wish, like stars we soar,
In this moment, we ask for more.

The sun sets low, painting the scene,
With hues of gold, and soft serene.
A festival of dreams takes flight,
In the glow of the fading light.

With each heartbeat, fervor grows,
Embracing joy as the river flows.
Hold on tight, through the ups and downs,
In unity, we wear our crowns.

Let courage guide, with spirits high,
In every heart, the love will fly.
To dance like leaves on the warmest breeze,
This flight of heart, an endless tease.

Emotions Unbridled

Gathered round, the fires glow,
Stories shared, the laughter flows.
In the day's sweet, tender end,
A chorus of joy, together we blend.

Footsteps echo on soft, green ground,
With every leap, we are unbound.
Colors splash like paint on a wall,
In this carnival, we rise, we fall.

Bounce like children, let spirits roam,
Through the night, we find our home.
With every cheer, the moments collide,
In our hearts, emotions untried.

Soak in the magic, let love unfold,
A tapestry of memories, pure gold.
Through laughter and tears, let's hold tight,
In this journey, our hearts take flight.

The Call of Open Skies

Hear the echoes of joy so bright,
Under the moon, we share delight.
With every breeze, whispers commence,
Calling us forth, so rich, so dense.

Moments spark, like fireworks bright,
We dance in rhythm, hearts taking flight.
Together we roam through the vast unknown,
In the land of dreams, we feel at home.

The stars awake, a wondrous sight,
In the stillness, everything feels right.
Breathe deeply now, let worries fly,
In the freedom of night, our spirits lie.

So raise your glass, toast to the skies,
In this celebration, love never dies.
With laughter and music, we find our prize,
Heeding forever, the call of open skies.

Tides of Passion

The waves dance bright under the moon,
Laughter and music fill the night soon.
Colors of joy swirl in the air,
Hearts beat together, love flows everywhere.

In the warmth of the fire, tales unfold,
Each whisper and smile worth more than gold.
With every toast, our spirits do soar,
Celebrate the moments we all adore.

As stars twinkle high, we dream and we sing,
Life's vibrant rhythm makes our souls spring.
With hands held tight, we step into bliss,
Sharing this magic, a collective kiss.

The tide pulls us close, we're never apart,
In this wave of joy, we open our heart.
Let's ride this tide, let it carry us high,
As passions ignite, together we fly.

Breaking the Mold

Bright banners sway with the morning breeze,
New dreams arise, putting minds at ease.
Colorful bursts of laughter and cheer,
We break the mold, let our spirits steer.

The rhythm of life dances wild and free,
In a world of wonders, just you and me.
Together we leap, away from the grey,
Embracing the moments, come what may.

With each fresh step, we pave our own way,
In this vibrant story, we choose to play.
The light of our hearts shines bright on this road,
This festive journey is ours to explode!

So lift up your voice, let the joy unfold,
In this celebration, we break from the old.
With hands intertwined, we'll conquer and climb,
In every heartbeat, we find our own rhyme.

Horizons Welcoming Hope

Golden rays paint the dawn's soft embrace,
Together we smile, as light starts to grace.
Hope dances boldly, like flowers in bloom,
With every new day, we banish the gloom.

The horizon whispers, beckoning us near,
With dreams yet to chase, we have nothing to fear.
We rise with the sun, hearts open and wide,
In the warmth of each moment, together we stride.

Mountains and rivers, adventures await,
On this path of joy, let's celebrate fate.
Each step brings us closer, let laughter ignite,
As we journey forward, our future is bright.

So gather around, let us cherish the now,
With hope in our hearts, we'll ignite the vow.
Horizons inviting, new stories to find,
In this festive spirit, we're wondrously blind.

The Spirit's Voyage

A ship sails softly on waters that gleam,
With sails full of laughter, we follow the dream.
The compass of joy points us toward light,
In unity rising, we embrace the night.

Friends by our side, and the stars overhead,
With melodies weaving, our hearts are well-fed.
Each wave we conquer unites us as one,
On this joyous voyage, we'll never be done.

The wind carries whispers of tales yet untold,
We navigate the tides, both daring and bold.
With every soft splash, memories unfold,
This festive spirit will never grow old.

As we chart our course to horizons anew,
The treasure is joy; together, it's true.
Our spirits will sail through each laughter and tear,
On this voyage of life, forever sincere.